JOURNEY MY HEART

A COLLECTION OF POETRY

LATAVYA FOSTER

JOURNEY MY HEART
Copyright © 2016 by (LaTavya Foster)

All rights reserved. No Portion of this book may be reproduced, scanned, or distributed in any printed or electronic form without written permission of the author, with the exception of brief excerpts for magazine articles, reviews, etc. For further information or permission, write to poetjustay@gmail.com

ISBN-10 :978-0-9890787-4-0
ISBN-13: 978-0-9890787-4-0
Published by: Voices of Zion LLC
Cover design: Isabella Gonzalez
Photo editing: Jim Osareniye, JimStone Productions
Photo by: Harun Jibri "Gabreal Lyrix" Donaldson, JIDONcompany

Printed in USA

Dedication:

In loving and treasured memory of my momma,
♥ *Angela Foster (1969-2016)*♥

For your love and support and strength, I love you, and I patiently await the day when I, again, can see your face, kiss your cheeks, and do that stroke along your arm that you said annoyed you. I love you.

Table of Contents

Acknowledgements 5
Introduction 7
Empty Tomb 8
Galatians 2:20 10
Cancer Conquered 12
Spiritual Warfare 14
Straddler 16
Death 18
Looking Back 19
Pressing Forward 21
Free 23
13th Amendment 25
Our Lives Matter 28
Freedom is Big 31
Woman 34
Imperfectly Perfect 35
Bitch is NOT my name 38
Man 40
Unsafe 43
Silent Cries 45
Justin: I Choose You 47
Sisters in Christ 49
Love Making 52
Muse 56
What If 57
If Only He Knew 59
Hold him 60
Undedemwen (EMBRACE) 61
Love Sought 63
Keep on Holding On 68
Here is Christ 71
Jesus 73

Acknowledgments

1 Peter4:10-11 NLT - God has given each of you a gift from His great variety of spiritual gifts. Use them well to serve one another. Do you have the gift of speaking? Then speak as though God Himself were speaking through you. Do you have the gift of helping others? Do it with all the strength and energy that God supplies. Then everything you do will bring glory to God through Jesus Christ. All glory and power to Him forever and ever! Amen.

I thank the one and only true living God, first and foremost, for His faithfulness, His amazing grace, and His unfailing love. I am thankful that it pleased God to entrust me with the gifts of speaking and writing and to use me as His vessel of encouragement and inspiration. God be praised and glorified, for without Him, none of this would be. He has granted me favor.

I thank Osagie Omorowa, owner of VOICES OF ZION, LLC for his support, his patience, his advice, and his gentle nudges during this project. Thank you for believing in me so much so that you don't mind attaching your name to this project. SMILE. Thank you for your prayers.

To my poet societies, SAY THAT (founded by Thomas "T-Nu" Newell) and WE GIVE YOU PRAISE (founded by Warnell "DaBear" Caldwell). I thank God for acquainting me with such like-minded,

Kingdom-minded individuals. I love each of all of yall. Thank you, Haran Jibri "Gabreal Lyrix" Donaldson, for assisting me in this process.

To my Grace Temple family. Man, I can only smile and bless God for all the support and encouragement you've given me. Ms. Linda Jackson, you are my boo thang, despite you always putting me on the spot. SMILE. Diana Morrison, you my boo thang, too, and my ride or die, in the name of Jesus, of course. LOL. Janice Thompson, I love you, woman!! Ha, I get to call you by your first name because this is my book. SMILE.

Thank you to Micheal Guinn (founder of FORT WORTH POETRY SLAM), Brenda Randall (Host of Poetry Smash and founder of IN THE WORDS OF A SISTAH), and Tina Turner Young (founder of VOICE) for allowing me to step foot on your stages time and time and time again. I am grateful.

To my family and friends, thank you for your love, support and encouragement.

If I failed to acknowledge anyone, please charge it to my head, not my heart.

Introduction:

They ask me what I am, and I tell them, "I am a poet."
When asked what I do, I say, "I write, and I spit."
When asked why I do it, I simply respond, "Obedience."

The believers are called to ... publish His glorious deeds among the nation. Tell everyone about the amazing things He does (Psalms 96:3 NLT).

It is true that there are times even the strongest of us need to be reminded of God's love for us, His faithfulness toward us, and that God is still in control. Other times, we need to be reminded of our worth. In between times, we need encouragement, uplift, and hope, and every now again, we need some knowledge poured into us. And it doesn't hurt to have a little glimpse of romantic love sprinkled along our way.

The pages of this book portray all of these things. It is my prayer that you finish this book with a desire to know God more, possess a deeper sense of worthiness, and love those with whom you come in contact.

Empty Tomb
Mat 26-28, Isa 53:5

Because sin conceived me
And iniquity shaped me
You were sent here to save me

And it was in Gethsemane,
with a heart filled with sorrow,
That you gave up your will
For the Father's will
So that I may see a hopeful tomorrow.
But where was your intercessor?

But you knew
That only you
Could save us
So you drank from that cup.
Though it was my transgressions that wounded you,
And my iniquities that bruised you,
It was Calvary that held you
When you hung your head tasting death for me
My punishment was upon your head
like the thorns your crown carried.
Numbered with transgressors and buried amidst the wicked.
Your countenance afflicted
From the wrong I had committed.
The weight of my guilt was upon you,

But you
You – guiltless
You – faultless
You – sinless

But now the wage for my sin left on
that cross.
Your blood - my redemption
Your death, my salvation.

And while I was yet a sinner, you died for me
And even in the midst of my transgressions, you came to save me.
And though my faults had beaten and pierced you, you forgave me.
Though Satan tried to stop you,
And sin tried to subdue you,
Death tried to end you,
Even the grave tried to keep you.
But nothing could hold you
And so you
Rose for me.

And it's for this reason that I stand for you,
Proclaiming that as for me and my house, we will serve you.
Going all the way with you.
No day without you.
Leaving behind my backsliding
No more hiding
Behind the excuse
That I'm only human.
And because you laid down your life for me
I'll lift you up before men.
And I'll give you all the glory, honor,
and praise.
Because even though I didn't deserve it.
You still did it.
You died for me.
You paid the price for me.
You gave eternal life to me.
So wherever you go,
I will follow.
Wherever you lead,
There I'll be

Galatians 2:20

There dwells a certain enthusiasm
A sort of fascination
A passion
Within us
For Christ

A conscious decision
A willful submission
An unquestionable conviction
To give God our lives
Because Christ, He gave His for us.

Remembering the cross
With a full confidence
A blessed assurance
That Christ, He loves us
His passion for us is obvious

So no longer I who live, but Christ who lives in me.
No longer worldy pleasures or selfish desires
No longer pride
Those have been denied.
No longer enslaved
To corruptible ways
Because I have died.

By faith, I live in this flesh – inherent sinfulness
In this world, but not of it.
In this flesh, but not lusting after it.
By faith, I surrender my will to His will – perfect and flawless
By grace, I am changed!
Pardon for sins obtained!
Eternal salvation arranged!

No longer I
But Christ

Pause for the Cause

Before proceeding to the next piece, be informed that I have not battled cancer, but I know of many who have battled the pestilence, and God has shown favor and grace and provided healing to their bodies, and now they are living victorious lives in the absence of cancer. This piece is dedicated to those who are battling and who have battled cancer. God has the final word. Believe the report of the Lord.

Cancer Conquered
Psa 91, Prov 4:20-22

This here has become war
The moment you made my body your residence
Without my consent,
You summoned my inner strength.

See, this has become a war.
You thought you came to battle against just a corruptible entity
But in all reality
You battle not against just lil ole me,
But against my whole purpose,
Against my whole reason to be.
See, you thought this conquest would be easy
You came with defeat as your mission
But I claimed victory
Over you and your intentions

But still, you wanted to fight.
How much stronger did you think you were than God's promises
To deliver me from your pestilence
I fought the good fight of faith
Every day I looked into your face
But you, you miscalculated the power of God's word
That long life shall he satisfy me
That because I have set my love on Him, he will deliver me
That one thousand shall fall at my side
And ten thousand at my right hand
But it shall not come near me; so, here I stand.

Because I am thoroughbred

Created from the purest and the best
When he blew his breath into my nostrils,
Endurance
Persistence
And resilience
Flowed through me indomitably.

So, with every piece of my life's quality that you took
My will to sustain increased that much more
And every treatment that made we weaker
Pushed me closer to restoration than I was the day before
Every time I cried out to God, He heard me
Every time I turned my ear to His word, they become health to my body
Every time I prayed and believed
I received

So yeah, you forced me in the valley of the shadow of death
But when we got there, you were not expecting Omnipotence
You were not expecting God to show up with his rod of protection and his staff of guidance
You were not expecting Goodness and Mercy to follow me all the days of my life
You were not expecting me to survive.

But for my life, I will fight.
Christ didn't tap out.
And since I am made in His image, neither will I

Spiritual Warfare
2Cor 4:8-9, Eph 6:10-17

The powers of darkness are waging war
Against those who seek after our Lord.
This is real. This is no figment of our imagination.
Believers are a problem for Satan
And he seeks to take us with him to His eternal damnation.

This battle is real.
Aint no weapons of this world gone save you from this.
You gone need the weapons of God because these are not flesh and blood we battle with.

So by God's grace,
I will lay
Prostrate
Before the Lord night and day
Before I let the enemy have his way.
So, allow me to encourage you.

Grab prayer as your power
Take God's word
As your sword
And your faith as your shield
And don't you fret
We were already built for this.
God has already given us strength and courage for this.

We walk in victory
Over the enemy
Over all his intended destruction, his schemes, his trickery.
We walk in victory
So much so that we won't even hurt our feet.

And we don't have to wait until the end
To see who's gonna win.
Satan is already a defeated foe.
The Son of God, in His death and resurrection, has already eradicated the devil's works.
The one who destroys has now become the one who is destroyed.
For God's word will not return to Him void.

So, satan, you can work your counterfeit miracles now
And you can boast in your deception now,
But you know who Christ is
You will be seen in all your wickedness
You will be confined to the gates of Hell
And you will not prevail.

You may press us from every which way
But we will not be crushed.
You may frustrate us
But we wont give up.
You can hunt us down, but God will not abandon us.
And even if you push us to the end of our rope
We will still have hope in us.

God is our defense.
And for those who love Him, He contends

So your weapons may form against us
But they will not prosper
Because through Jesus Christ, we are more than conquerors.

Straddler
1King 18:21

I
Had a fite
One night
With life
And he
Told me
That if I didn't get myself together spiritually,
That death would become me
Eternally.

C, I don't always practice what I preach,
But it's still God's word I teach.
And I always pray
That He keeps me safe
From the fiery darts of the adversary
Even though
I know
I'm rubbing elbows with the enemy.
In front of the church folk, I replace swearing and cursing
With words of edification and purpose.
Cause I wouldn't dare
Air
My dirty laundry
For them to judge me,
Condemn me,
And act like they're better than the likes of me.
So what, I turn up the bottle
More than I read from the Bible
My sins are silent
They're secret

So, I looked at Life
Square dead in his eyes
"You are wasting your time.
I uphold most of what God says so I'm definitely not on the Devil's side.
Death will never know me.
The closest I'll get to death is sleep.
I honor my mother and father, never used the Lord's name in vain.
And I am a Christian, I'll quickly proclaim.
I'm not a murderer, not a thief
Don't want nothing somebody else got, I'm not committing adultery.
See, I got black rims on my black navigator
Wearing shoes made out of alligator
Matching Gucci with Gucci cause I aint no perpetrator.
How could I be doing it like that
If Death was riding my back?"

So without responding, Life left me
Right there in the back seat.
My black navigator now a black hearse
And I can't plead deliverance from this eternal curse.
I'm screaming,
But seems
Noone hears me
"Lord, Lord, haven't I done it all in Your name
Havent I done it all for Your sake"
But He responded that He never knew me
Now, death has become me
Eternally.

Death
Romans 8:13

It would be unforgivably careless, even loveless of me to come before you
And not inform you
That no matter what you do
There has to be death.

It's an inevitable truth.
One cannot avoid
Death's cord.

If you waver too long between two opinions, you will lose your life.
And even if you are crucified with Christ, you will still have to die
To self.
So no matter which way you choose, there will be death.

Eternal death as a stipend for your sin
Or you give up your life because, now, it's no longer you who live, but Christ who lives within.
And if I could suggest which path you should take,
I'd steer you toward the only name by which you can be saved.
Christ!
For through Him, there is life beyond the grave.
Here is His mercy. Here is His grace –
Where we should have died, Christ stepped in and took our place
And for that reason alone, I choose to die to my flesh every day.

"Well done, my good and faithful servant." Isnt that what you want to hear the Lord say.
But if don't, you will taste eternal death
For yourself.
As for me, I choose to die
So I can live in Christ.

Looking Back
Psa 77:5-12

People tell us to leave our past behind us,
That in order to move forward, we must stop looking backwards.
That we cannot progress unless we are focused on what's ahead of us
This is true in some cases.

But I use my past as a reminder
Not to linger
But as a reminder that things got better
That my failings didn't make me a failure
That I became stronger, wiser

My past is a reminder that trouble won't last always
That after sleepless nights come joyful days
My past is saturated with testimony
I am filled because I came to Him empty
I brought Him my brokenness
And He gave me His wholeness
I know His rest because I've been burdened
I know His peace because I've been hurt and troubled

And back is where Gethsemane is
Where Christ's sweat was like drops of blood,
where he shed tears
Back is where the Cross is
Back is where our invitation to eternity was given
Where His resurrection equaled our salvation

So, I encourage you to remember your past
Not as a hindrance, but as a reminder

Remember
That when you were weak, He became your strength
When you were prisoner to transgressions, He was your deliverance
When you were in need, He was your provider
When you were afflicted in your body, He was your healer
Look back and remember so that when you're waiting for results longer than you want to
Or when you feel like God isn't hearing or listening to you
You'll be reminded that God is the same yesterday, today, and tomorrow
That if he does not another thing for you, He's done plenty
Already

So thank Him for your past
Praise Him because you see a difference when you look back
I don't have ten thousand tongues to thank Him, but with my one tongue, I'll praise Him ten thousand plus times
Because on His back are the stripes
In His hands are the holes and I won't forget that in His side, he was stabbed
So never forget your past.

Pressing Forward
Romans 5:3-4

I'm pressing forward though my situation wants me
To believe
That it gets no better
And I'm still holding on even though
My will wants me to let go
But I know better
Because giving up or giving in
Is not an option
Because then, the devil wins
And unfortunately for him, my God is quite the competitor
So, this race
That has been placed
Before me
At my feet
I'll continue to run
From the waking of the sun
Until the moon rests its head
Even until the day that my body lies dead
I'll be at His feet
Pleading His mercy
Because He invited me
To come before His throne boldly.

Pause for the Cause

You know, every now and again, I want to discuss some things Black. I love my Black, and I count it as a blessing to be covered in such rich melanin. We are exactly how God made us to be.

In our history, we see years of struggle with slavery and overt discrimination, and in our present chapter, we see the establishment and growth of racism. There is history that is not taught in the textbooks. There are perspectives on injustice that are not voiced. So allow me to pause for the cause of sharing my heart and providing some facts about where we've been and where we stand today.

Free

I used to be a slave, bound by inequality, suffering and pain,
Longing for a day when all of this insanity would change.
When the whelps on my back would symbolize survival.
When the word Master would refer only to the Lord and Savior.
When I'd no longer be forced to labor.

When my moaning
Would evolve into rejoicing.
When I'd become my own voice and
I deposited my hope into times when my drenching sweat and sorrowful tears
Would demolish the gates of struggle and fears.
When the soil of this land would signify we've overcome
Rather than remain a reminder that we're victim.

I envisioned the day when captivity
Would be only a part of our history
When my lineage would know how it felt to be free.

See, I aint who I use to be
Bondage no longer knows me
Slave no longer my name
Honey, I've got rights to claim.
I've traded my ignorance for knowledge and literacy.
Potential has displaced impossibilities.
My desperation
Replaced with motivation.
My struggle laid to rest

Understand that we are a people of vision,

Establishment
Accomplishment
A people with a mission.

So, embrace yourselves
The only boundaries are those you place upon yourselves
Be brave, be empowered, be beautiful
Be strong, be exceptional

And I know believing in the liberty we've longed for
Has gotten me called naïve and gullible
Heck, I've been called much worse, some I was okay with
But there were some I hated,
I've been Nigger, I've been Negro, Colored, Now, they call me Black,
Call me
What you please,
Just be sure you remember that I am **FREE**!

13th Amendment

1776
Declaration of Independence –
We hold these truths to be self-evident
That all men are created equal
But what was not stated, yet later understood, is that this equality
Applied only to the white men who were free
So, you, my black friend
You have too much melanin
And you, with your wide hips and your big lips, your hair is too nappy
So, you are no more than a slave, you are mere property.
Slave and human do not mean the same thing.

1863
Emancipation Proclamation
All persons held as slaves within the Confederacy
Shall be forever free
Except
Because there is always an exception
Some sort of exclusion
Except you slaves in 13
Of Louisiana's parishes and New Orleans
You are still in possession
But don't fret, you'll be in good company
Because the Union slaves will also still be
In custody
Lincoln freed some slaves but he didn't outlaw slavery completely.

So, hence,
1865 – the 13th Amendment

If you are not convicted of a crime, no slave
Or involuntary servant shall exist in the United States

But let's pause here.
Because here is where our reality becomes the untold
Where the bad and the ugly unfold
Where you discern that everything that glitters isn't gold

See, the original intent
Of the 13th amendment
Was to make slavery constitutional and permanent.
Receiving 3/4s of the votes in both the House and the Senate
And gaining support for Lincoln, you know him – our favorite President.
But before all states could consent
The Civil War commenced
So I guess we should give a grand ole salute to political greed
For setting us free.

But what I don't understand and what I want explained to me is
America, are you blindly following your forefathers' constructs?
Or is it the media that makes you hate us?
Is it propaganda that serves as the basis for your bias?
Or do you just really believe you were born as a racist?

Because I, I was born Black and though I wear my Black proudly
I know that it will take more than an "I Have a Dream Speech"
And more than President Obama as Commander in Chief

More than #BLACK LIVES MATTER and #I CANT BREATHE
More than some poems and songs revealing your bigotry

But I...Am...Black
And I am Black unapologetically.
I will be Black all up in your face
I will be Black all up and through your space
And if I could die and come back,
I'd come back Black
And if my Black offends you,
Then you should leave the room.
I will defend my Black, I will fight for my Black
And if my Black becomes the death of me
Then, so shall it be.

Our Lives Matter

All lives matter? To God, yes they do..
But to the mother of three black boys, the only lives I really care about are the ones I gave birth to.
And the ones who look like them.
Because they, the whites, they already have undeniable privilege on their side
But my boys, your boys, our cousins,
nephews, uncles, fathers, our husbands,
They need someone to care about their lives.

Because it's clear that some of these hired to protect and serve the communities
Have set an agenda to harass, beat, and kill certain ethnicities.
And by certain ethnicities, I mean blacks.
With each dead unarmed black male, it becomes a more obvious fact
That they don't want us here.
And any excuse they can use to pull the trigger
Is condoned because the victim was just some other nigger.
Because to them, our lives don't matter.

So, this "all lives matter" is the biggest blank faced lie if I ever heard one
Sounds to me like America is diminishing its problem
That blacks are a target
America wants us to believe that whites, they have the same struggle.

And they don't.

They don't know how it feels to pray day in and day out
That your sons make it back to the house
The same way they left
Unharmed, uninjured, and not dead
They don't know how it feels to panic when 7:30 is what the clock shows
And you were expecting your babies 30 minutes ago.

They don't know what it's like to have to remind your asthmatic son
That "Son, if a cop pulls you over, I need you to stay calm.
I don't want you reaching for your asthma pump
Because then, son, they'll say you were reaching for a gun.
And son,
No matter what happens, no matter how afraid you are, you never run.
"Hands up. Plain sight. Don't speak
Don't move. Don't reach."

And I don't know if I should teach my black sons to approach a cop if they're in danger.
Because the way things are, they'd probably be better off with their attacker.
At least then, I can pay a ransom.

They don't have to teach their sons that sometimes, you have to surrender your ego, your pride
Just to stay alive.
They don't have to explain propaganda and stereotypes.
They're not having these types of conversations.
Because they don't have to face racial subordination.
But we have to continuously validate and encourage our babies

Because we know that we are considered lower than the lowest whites because of our color.
We know that racism is permanent and indestructible.

So, hell no, they don't know our struggle.

We marched 50 years ago and here we are again.
Having to do the same thing
Protest night and day
Just to put this problem in America's face.

Because now, instead of a rope around our necks,
We get a bullet through our chest.
Instead of "Whites Only" signs
We get "Black Unarmed Boy killed by Police" in our headlines.

So, America, if all lives matter, if all lives are worth saving,
Why, then, is black blood becoming your new pavement?

Our Lives Matter, too!

Freedom Is Big

June nineteenth isn't the day that the Negro was freed.
It's the day they told us we were no longer obligated to their captivity
June nineteenth isn't the day that the Negro was freed.
It's the day that they decided enough harvesting was complete

"The connection heretofore
Existing between them becomes that between employer
And free laborer"

Ah, freedom – the ability to act, live as you see fit
Live as you wish
Without confinement, with restriction

This is a big deal. Freedom is big.

Freedom is big
Big like being Commander in Chief
Like being 1st lady of this "land of the free."
Big like being recognized for our contributions
Big like making history.

Freedom is big
Big like coming together, shutting down highways to march and protest
Big like giving ourselves privilege
Like fighting to keep our freedom and protect it.

Freedom is big
Big like education and knowledge is a must

Like picking up books and reading, not just to sit on a shelf and collect dust

Freedom is big
Big like financial independence, economic security
Like discouraging riots and looting so we can protect our own economy
Like having our court system hold police at greater accountability
Freedom is big like responsibility

Freedom is big
Big like passing through the shadow of the valley of death time and time again
And still standing
Like realizing that slavery was a struggle
Indeed, but it progressed us.
Big like grasping potential
Like ignoring the media's agenda
To push propaganda
Big like challenging stereotypes
Big like united we stand, together we fight

Freedom is big
Big like resilience
Big like strength

Freedom is big.
Big like it belongs to us.

Pause For the Cause

Say, my ladies, I love yall!

Have I told you how much I love being a woman?! Well, I looooove being woman!! And as a woman, I realize the perceived vulnerabilities associated with our gender — we love easily, we are seen as the weaker sex, we get impatient waiting for the right guy and we settle, we are more susceptible to disrespect, and the list continues. But by the grace of God, we don't have to model or live our lives under such deceptions and stereotypes. I bear witness of God's amazing grace. I am no longer victim to insecurities. I no longer lack standards. I realized my worth in Christ, trusted God, and walked away from domestic violence. PRAISE BREAK for deliverance from domestic violence!!!

We are all beautiful, each in our own unique way. We each have something to offer this universe. There is enough sun to shine on each of us and enough road to travel our journeys and reach our destinations. So, by the grace of God, let us lift and hold each other up, empower each other. Let us love each other.

Let us respect ourselves and require respect from others. We are honorable; so, require honor.

Ladies, you are beautiful, strong, and intelligent. Even if I do not know you personally, I know the God who made you, and He makes no mistakes. You are wonderfully made!!!

You need no validation from man. The Word of God already validates you.

Woman!

God broke the mold when he made me
Those who have known peasantry appreciates the queen
No need to bow down, just respect my identity
You can keep your ordinary
There is nothing about your normal or your average that entices me
I am your life supply
I produce your lifetimes

I am both your before and your after
Both your right now and forever
I am she who can nurture nations
And she who will battle to save them
I am she who births your futures
She who can build and run a home and a corporation
She who is strength to an entire nature

I am WOMAN!

Imperfectly Perfect

Men have a long list of ways they want us to be
They want our throats deep
They want our Maybelline on fleek
They want us to have hair that flows like satin sheets
Full lips, better to grip them with.
Full hips, better for them to grip.
They want our nails freshly manicured every time they see us
Every time we go somewhere, they want us in 5 inch pumps
Want us thin in the waist
Want us to wake up with no sleep in our eye
And our breath smelling like springtime
They want a bust that reminds them of Playboy Bunnies
And a butt so big they can sit their drink on it.
They want a whole lot of stuff from us

And so the cycle begins
Trying to be the most perfect, the baddest female he's ever seen.
So a little niptuck here.
Botox there
Remove a couple ribs
Injection to make that bigger
Waist trainer
Transfer fat
From this to that

The cycle begins
And she still won't win
Because when she looks in her mirror, she can't recognize herself
Not much of how God made her is left.

But it continues
Because she thinks this is what's needed to get and keep this dude.
But honey, he aint worth it.

But still, instead of learning to handle the family budget,
Or just sew a button
She's learning to twerk on command.

Instead of reading a book
Or finishing school,
She's learning to pole dance with no hands.
And it's all for ole dude

My friend, invest in your independence
And your self-confidence
More than you invest in some fraud of a man.

Because he
He is just the opposite of what your husband should be
He is not what you need.

What complements you
Is the man who chooses you simply because you are you

Now don't get me wrong, we all want a looker, somebody we can at least stomach.
But ladies, we are more than our hair, our lips,
We are more than our booty and our tits.
We're more than our dancing abilities, and we are more than our clits.

We are class.
We are cultivated minds.
We are strength and sacrifice
We are truth, love and loyalty,
Consistency and honesty.
We are foundation builders
We are go-getters

And though we have flaws and imperfections, we are made wonderfully
Miraculously
Intricately
Individually sculpted by the hand of God
We are beautiful just the way we are

So, ladies, give your energy to the man who chooses you
For more than your physical attributes
Because that man, that man will stay
Even after everything else loosens, sags and fades.

Pause for the Cause

The poem on this next page may seem offensive to some because of its repeated use of a particular profane word. It is not my intention to offend you by including such a piece. The intent of this poem is to challenge how some women allow men to use such profane labels toward us. Some women feel empowered or exclusive when labeled as such, but such a label is derisive. We cannot allow men to talk to us any kind of way.

A wise older lady once told me, "If you don't demand it, they won't supply it. And if you keep accepting it, they have no reason to change it."

While the piece makes use of a foul word, I do not consider this piece ungodly. This is not to say that I condone the use of foul language. God has called us to speak only words of edification and life, to affirm the dignity of every person. This piece does not come from a heart of contempt or frustration; rather, the setting is a heart of regard and love in an attempt to correct and redirect.

Bitch Is NOT My Name

He approached me in all innocence
Thinking he was giving me a compliment
He gawked at me from my feet to my hips
From my hips to my chest to my lips
And parting his lips, he told me I was a bad bitch.
And the anticipation etched in his smile
Suggested that he was awaiting a reply
But I didn't have one.
At least not the one he would want
See, the typical female may have received a boost to her confidence
But I am not impressed with
Nor do I entertain ignorance.
I was not moved.

And I guess that blasé look on my face
Now gave him reason to use the same word for disgrace
By calling me a siddity bitch
Then he walked away.

He approached yet another queen
And told her the same thing
"You are a bad bitch"
And her smile met his.

Now, I could just leave this piece at that and hope you get the message
But if you're impressed with being called a bitch
Then you won't get this.
So, now I have to explain
That there is nothing romantic about being called out of your name.

In less than 30 seconds, the same word he used to impress me
He, now, used to oppress me

But you want to reclaim it?!
You want to embrace it.

And why?
Because you think words don't matter
But if ole white girl was to call you a nigger, you'd square up at her.

So assert yourself at him, too.
Demand he gives you the respect and honor due you.

The independence you exude when you think for yourself
The truth you speak even when honesty is feared by everyone else
And the strength and ambition you radiate
The class and confidence your display
The courage you project when you stand against the things that are wrong
Don't let him diminish those qualities to some four legged female dog

When he sees you as a bitch, you're not being set a part.
That's not some title he's given only you because you hold a special space in his heart.
Every female he comes across is some kind of bitch to him.
A real, worthy man uses respect and dignity to address women

And if you were to turn right around and call him a bitch,
Well, you'll find yourself back handed, maybe even kicked.

Are yall getting it?

The last time I checked, none of us humped hydrants.

Man

The definition of a man is not determined by the width of his shoulders
Nor by how many women at one time he can juggle
That makes him an adulterer.
And just because he mows the lawn and takes out the trash
And can count all six packs of his abs
He is still not a man.

Defining a man is not in the firmness of his handshake
And believe it or not, it's not even in the amount of money he makes
And just because he sits on the couch with his hands
In his pants
That still does not make him a man
In fact, that makes him nasty.

And don't think that just because he doesn't ask for directions, he's a man; perhaps, a stronger one
No, honey, that just makes the trip a longer one.

The definition of a man is not even determined by how big
His EGO is

And let's just clarity confusion so we'll understand
Pumping testosterone makes him a male, not a man.

So, I'll explain
So it can be plain
What it is that makes a man

Consider
His character
Humble is a man

Realizing that he doesn't always have to be right
That it is okay to not be so dominant all the time.
He understands he has two ears and one mouth for a reason
Because a man knows that he learns more by listening than by speaking

Men recognize that it's okay to not know
Because walking by faith takes balls

Optimism shields a man.
Never giving up and never giving in
Cha cha'ing his way all the way to his dream
Life pulls him forward
Then knocks him back
Forward again
And then back once more
But a man
He doesn't mind a dance

A man is comfortable in his own skin
He is covered in confidence
While carrying your purse
Crying at church
All while wearing a pink shirt

A man doesn't play games
Always saying what he means
And meaning what he says
His momma taught him that if he'll lie
He'll steal, and if he steals,
He'll kill.
He'd rather not be associated with the mere appearance
Of fraudulence
So a man, he keeps his promises

Gentle is a man
Polite in his words and his actions, never speaking aggressively
Never raising his hands violently
Because he was taught that his hands are for hugging and for working
Not for hitting, smacking or choking

Faithful is a man
Rather than doing many women wrong, he finds joy in doing one woman right.
He knows that he has found a good thing when he has found a wife.

And on that note, respect girds a man
Just because our idea of a nightcap
Doesn't involve us sitting naked on your lap
Doesn't mean we're not into you
It means we have standards, and perhaps, you should get some, too.

A man, above all else, keeps the charge of the Lord, our God.
Walking in all His ways and keeping His commands.
So do as David told Solomon, "Be strong, therefore, and prove yourself a man."

Unsafe

Every day she wore long sleeves, dark glasses and heavy makeup
Because she needed to hide the bruises, the black eyes, and avoid those questions they'd ask her
Like, "What'd you do to provoke him?"
As if whatever she did justified his hands clenching her neck until she was left near breathless
Or him kicking, shaking or slapping her until she was left helpless
He's the aggressor
Why not hold him accountable?

He told her that whenever he wanted it, she had to give or he'd just take it.
And since she had committed her life to being his wife, she felt obligated.
"Submit!" they said, "after all, he is your husband."
"That's not rape," they said, "You're just fulfilling your marital covenant."
But they were misinformed. Someone told them wrong
Because taking his last name does not negate your right to say no.

He never hit her with his hands
Why would he when his words could cut deeper than any knife can.
He was a master at making her question her adequacy
At diminishing her independence while broadening her insecurities
"You shut up, you dumb broad, you low life fool!"
"You ought to be grateful because aint nobody else gonna want you!"
Night and day she heard these words
And she believed them because she forgot her worth.

Now ladies, I know they say that giving up makes us weak.
But in an unsafe home, giving up keeps us from being six feet deep.
We don't ask for abuse, and we don't deserve it either.
Whatever we did or did not do, it does not matter
Because his hands were made to wipe away your tears
To pull you in close, hold you tightly so you know someone cares
His feet were made for walking, to support him as he supports you.
His tongue was made for edification
To speak words of love and patience

And if he uses his hands, feet or tongue for any other reason.
Pack your bags and leave him.

Silent Cries

This is for the ladies who keep silent about their abuse
Whose cries go unheard
Whose wounds are invisible

You are not alone. There is help.
You don't have to do this by yourself
And I won't try to convince you to leave
Because I know leaving is not that easy
But I will challenge you to look in the mirror

And remember
The beautiful, lovely girl you were
Before this fool came in and shook your world
I will challenge you to not let a man treat you in a way you wouldn't approve for your baby girl

Ive heard it said, "If things start to go wrong, don't go with them."
So I want you to know that you cannot change him.
His actions are not your fault. He's to blame.
It won't get any better.
It will take more than just one more prayer.
It will take more than you reinventing yourself into what he wants because he will never be satisfied.
Besides, you are already a matchless prize

The reality of it is that no matter what you do
No matter what you don't do
His abuse will continue

So, I pray that you become sick and tired real soon.
I pray that you wake up one day and say no more

That you gain the strength, the courage, the faith you need to pack your bags and head out the door
Never to return
I pray that one day sooner than later, no one will have to encourage you to leave
Because you'll love yourself so much that making him history
Will come naturally
And I pray that when you are ready to love again,
You will look back at this experience
Not to dwell there, but to motivate you never to repeat it.

(PRAISE BREAK because I know God will do it for you! He did it for me!!)

Justin: I Choose You

When I chose you, I chose heartache.
Even chose worse and sickness over goodness' sake.
I knew that calling you mine would be hell to pay.
I already knew that there would be unnecessary fights
About who has what rights.
I knew that this negro would be in my life
For the rest of your life.
But still, I chose you..

For every contraction I felt during labor
I knew regret would forever be my neighbor.
On that hospital bed, when I gave you his last name,
I already knew this family wouldn't be as pretty as the one in that new frame.
The yucky diapers and the sleepless nights, I was ready for.
Convincing you to eat veggies
Teaching you not to give your friends wedgies
Those I could handle
Praying over you and for you and with you.
That I could do.

But there was no advise, no book, no pamphlet
That could prepare me for all the years you'd be missing from your favorite blanket
When I chose you, I thought I was choosing right
You know, by choosing pro-life.
But giving you life has brought emptiness to me
A former happiness in me that has yet to be retrieved.
So, 8 years and counting, I still don't know where you are.
Because when I chose you, I chose that bastard as your father.
So now I spend my nights lying prostrate
And my days praying
That he'll bring you home
Where you belong.

But when I chose you, I chose God's way.
So, without a doubt, I know you'll be home someday.
And if someday means that eternity has to show her face
Then I'll just keep my faith
At least that way,
I know you'll be home
Where you belong
In my arms
Because when I chose you,
I did what Christ would do.

Sisters in Christ

It pains me to see the current state of my bride,
As if the holes in my hands, and this piercing in my side
Was not enough.
My children, my daughters
How is it that you slaughter
Your sister with your angry words
And your abusive slurs?
And with that very same tongue, you want to bless me
How can you think that if you hate your sister, you can still love me?
And why the gossip?
If you want something to talk about, spread my gospel.
No need for jealousy
I've supplied from my riches each and every one of your needs.
So why must you compete?
It's all in vain, all in vain you worship me.

How do you call yourselves Christians
And you don't behave as one
Lacking compassion,
Lacking affection
Lacking love.
And who gave you the audacity to judge or condemn
Must I remind you that it's by my grace that you live.
And the righteousness that you think you have
Is still to me as filthy rags.

My God, hasn't my blood covered this
Covered all this foolishness?

You too have your imperfections
And you have your demons

You are all sinners
Why must you criticize her just because she's human.
Have I not commanded you to love your neighbor as you love yourself?
Have you not been told that abiding in love is above all else?
If she weeps, you weep.
When she rejoices,
You ought to rejoice more.
If she has problems,
Help her solve them.
When she is hurt, comfort her.
Even if she hurts you, forgive her.
If she is naked, clothe her.
If she hungers, feed her.
If she is discouraged,
Then encourage her.
If she is broken-hearted
Help her to mend it.
So why are your shoulders not soggy from her tears?
Why cant you see that you were her in recent years?

My bride, I want to bring more souls in to you
But your current state just won't do.
You'll run them off before they get to that first pew.
So take heed to what I tell you.
Your motives, your affections, let my Spirit renew.
Let my glory been seen upon you.
My bride, I love you.

I heard this cry from Heaven, and I don't know about you, but I wanna see my Redeemer's face in peace.
When he returns, I don't wanna be amongst those who are still asleep.

I wanna trade in the coldness of this world for the warmth
of his eternal love.
I wanna trade in my stained rags for a white robe.
I wanna give up my corruptibility
For his incorruptibility.
I want these former things to pass away.
No more hurt, no more death, no more pain.
I wanna live even though I die.
Wanna drink from that fountain of the water of life
And if you do not know how to love, God says he leads
even the blind by ways they have not known
And through unfamiliar paths, he'll guide us along.
And when we love our sisters exhaustlessly,
We display our love for GOD
And no eye has seen,
No ear has heard,
And no mind has conceived
What God has prepared
For those who love him.

Love Making

Okay, so listen
I met a guy the other day
He was coming my way
I was going his way
And then when we got far enough a-way
From each other, we turned and our eyes locked
But only for a moment because neither one of us wanted to get caught
Looking at the other
So we kept it moving
I figured that if he wasn't man enough to approach me
To let me know that he wanted to get to know me
Then deuces

Okay, but that's not the end
I ran into him again
He was coming my way
I was going his way
Then, our eyes locked
But this time we did get caught
Caught in a moment where normally
Carnality would overrule spirituality
And values and morals
Those would become boring
But he surprised me
He took me to a place where typically
Guys didn't take me
Down on my knees to pray
And he told me
That my heart should be so far hidden in God
That man has to seek God in order to find me
OMG

I was already in lust
And now I wanted him to make lust to me.

But he stopped me
Told me
That undefiled our bed must be.
But he still wanted to make love with me.
So, I was confused
So he clarified
He described
What he meant by lovemaking.

He told me that I could keep my words of empty flattery
That he'd rather hear words of love and incorruptibility
He wanted to appeal to me
Through morality
He asked me to flee all things WORLDly
So we could engage in all things WORDly.
He said instead of covering myself with tempting lingerie
I should cover myself with the breastplate of righteousness
And the shield of faith to defend us
Against the temptations that were lurking amongst us.
He told me to replace my thoughts of lust
With thoughts of purity
That to my bed he would not accompany me
But he would walk with me
Down the path that's straight and narrow
That if I wanted to impress him, I'd have to be one to follow
Every word that proceeds from the mouth of God
That in order to captivate him, I'd have to capture God's own heart.

He said he wouldn't kiss that tender part of my neck
He wouldn't even caress those other sensitive parts of my flesh.
But he would kiss my soul and caress my heart with patience, kindness, respect, loyalty
Instead of exploring my body
He'd rather explore God's word with me.
He said he wanted a woman of Proverbs 31, worth far more than rubies
And he wanted that woman to be me.

So, yes, I was impressed.
He said he wanted to make love
But not how he had done it in the past
He wanted to make love
But he wanted to make love last

So now I see the difference between ole dude I chased for me
And the man God designed for me.
See, ole dude, he's still trying to make lust to me.
But the man God designed, he makes love with me.

Pause for the Cause

How many of us still believe in pure, romantic love, the love that makes room for your imperfections?
And how many of us are scared of just the mention of love, afraid of it changing?

Well, by the grace of God, my ideas of love are being refined. I am unlearning everything I ever thought about love. I can attest that there is a challenge in believing that pure love exists. I've been stuck there, a sort of black hole, dodging every appearance of love, even avoiding situations that could open my heart to love, but the closer I drew to God, the more His grace allowed me insight about true love built on a firm foundation in God.

God is love and He gives us special grace to experience love, not just from Him, but from one another, the love between man and woman.

MUSE

She was his muse
Though he never spoke the words audibly
It resounded in his creativity
Each line he penned was filled with her beauty
She was his love poems

Every unique, vivid, carefully designed description
Was laced with the fruit apparent in her spirit
The rising rhythm symbolized his growing affection
The patterned arrangement portrayed his heart's connection
With her energy

Unlike his prose, he deemed her nothing ordinary.

Each space between his written words
Embodied the space he yearned
To close between himself and her

He loaded his poems with metaphors and similes
Seeking to reveal her essence adequately
His poems were a manifestation of the love he secretly harbored
He admired her
He loved her
He wanted to tell her
Instead he just wrote of her
So he could immortalize her

And he, he, too, was her love poetry
But, seemingly, a poem she'd never get to read.

What If...

She had trouble defining it
So she just kept on denying it
But it was obvious
As obvious as the Southern twang that danced off her tongue
She loved this man

She didn't understand the sensation she tried so discretely to conceal
Whenever he held her hand or gently caressed her ear.
Or the warmth that arose in her bosom
Whenever he told her how naturally her beauty blossomed.
When he whispered he loved her
Each time his arms swaddled her,
Unpacking her bags
All the while turning her disappointments into laughs.

Now, she knows what butterflies
Really feel like.

She wanted him for herself
If she could store him in a jar locked away under combinations
He'd be there, safely shielded from external admiration
Until the earth stopped completing rotations.

She wasn't sure if this was love
But whatever it was
It felt pure. It felt real. It felt God-sent.
The only other love she knew was battered and broken.
But this thing, this unfamiliar thing
She liked it.

She appreciated all her past heartbreaks, all her regrets
Because she felt those led her down the course where they met

She wears the smile that he gave her
He's her first thoughts
Her favorite phone calls
But her hardest prayers

She didn't choose him, her heart did
But its destiny, it's real. She's his rib.
But she's too traditional to reveal what she feels
So she carries on just wondering, "What if?"

If Only He Knew

I wonder does my demeanor tell it all
That the first time
I paid him mind,
My soul breathed, "Ahhh!"

I have petitioned the Most High to grace me to be his forever
I wonder if he's the reason my heart murmurs
I wonder if the pulse of his coratid
Matches the throb in my wrist
If his missing rib is the one inside me
Does he feel incomplete?

I wonder if he knows
That I want to create tender intimacy with him
The kind where I cradle myself between his legs
With my head Rested against his chest
Just so we can talk... and laugh... and study
Just so we can baptize ourselves in each other's company.

I wonder does he know
That I hear the beauty of truth when he speaks
When he's near, I can feel God's love, taste sweet serenity
That when he smiles, I see the opening of heaven
That he, in his essence,
Is a love poem.

He doesn't know
That I'd be daring enough to sketch I LOVE YOU through the flesh
of my flesh
Right underneath my left breast

He needs to know
That he causes me to write love
Say love
See love
Dream love
Speak love
Want love
His love.

Hold Him

If she could hold him, she'd hold him with her heart
If she used her arms, he'd know
That she never intended to let him go
She'd hold him just like she'd want to be held.
Like a binder holds the pages of her favorite book – securely
So tight that all of her "I's" become "we"

If she could hold him, she'd hold him in public, in private
As they sat in silence
She'd even hold him in her dreams
She'd hold him so closely
That it would be near impossible to distinguish
Her silhouette from his

If she could hold him, she'd hold him with her heart
Because though he is physically near, emotionally, they are worlds apart.

Udedemwen (EMBRACE)

If I could hold on just a while longer

Long enough
For his hug
To outlast
My wounded past

Just long enough
For his embrace
To replace
What's been stolen from me –
My love, my trust, my safety

To outlive
All my lacerated memories

I just want to rest in his arms
Just long enough to attain healing without leaving scars
To keep from falling apart
To immerse myself in his boldness and his humility
His strength, his loyalty
His gentleness, his purity
His beauty.

His hugs are like medication
None of the over-the-counter kind – it's that prescription
That can only come from the GREAT PHYSICIAN
His hugs feel like freedom from rejection, deliverance from insecurity
Feel like free therapeutic relief
His hugs steady my heartbeat

His hugs dismantle the triple-layered cemented barricade
Where my heart is encased.
His hugs interpret emotions that my words alone cannot express
His hugs are antidepressant, antianxiety, a reliever of stress

His hugs are long, lingering, both hands tight,
Makes me smile
Don't have to say a word
Kind of hugs

His hugs
Envelop me with acceptance
Acquaint me with resilience
Facilitate reassurance
I sense God's presence

His hugs
Feel like love
Feel like home

Love Sought

A collaboration effort with LaTavya "jusTay" Foster and Osagie Omorowa for the LOVE JONES EXPERIENCE

(Osagie) Yeah so I could get my Don Juan on and say some sensual like - my fingers long to read her arched spine like Braille as every thrust molds her moans, her moans make Mozart's melodies marvel at our sensual symphony and it's so majestic, it moves the midnight's moon to madness and provokes the stars to unhinge themselves from their intergalactic realm into the earth's gravitational pull, just to peer into our haven, just to take a closer look at this bright luminous light of ebony bodies flowing as one, Their essence is one - such a won-der. What is this?

Yeah, I could say that, but truth is I've seen relationships built on filthy fleshly feasts and bear no passion fruit, but prunes- left bitter, cold, and heartless. So lest that be my demise, I decline because such a design is deficient in delivering the true essence of love.

(LaTavya) Bitter, cold and heartless.
Wounded in the thick of impenetrable darkness.
Relationships do that.
Awaken the most intense desire
You never even knew you harbored.
Enticing you with uninhibited freedom that slaves only prayed about.
Just to leave you as a dependent captive that plantation owners bragged about.
I can do without that kind, the manual toil towards a dead end.
Relationships built on the potential of love – that's a fatal game of chance
And relationships, relationships are a game.
Competition,
Manipulation
Sexual yearnings and lustful cravings...disguised as romance

Relentless arguments, heartbreaking fights…masquerading as passion.
Unyielding exhaustion is what it is!
Why so much energy
For something that's so fleeting?
I'm over it.
Feels more like the reverberation of Judas' kiss.
Reminds me of malignant tumors – cancerous.
This cannot be love's true essence

(Both) And I want, I desire, I need real love

(Osagie) The love of a woman- who bears in her spirit the mutual conviction that our love is not one of just lip service, but of action.

(LaTavya) The love of a man - who leads with commitment, consistency, and honesty.
Who understands authentic intimacy
Who guards my heart just as he guards his own

(Osagie) and our bond so tight we keep others out that want to pervert it. So probity permeates the promise we professed to one another, and this is preciously prodigious because that means NO MATTER WHAT,

(LaTavya) and our affectionate connection so affluent,
So apparent that others who considered intrusion rethink it.
And our covenant
Becomes sealed with faithfulness and steadfast love
Because that means NO MATTER WHAT,

(Both) NO…MATTER…WHAT

(Both) we will choose for love to be secured in warmth in the bitter winters, seek support in the storms of spring, keep our union irrigated in the searing summers, and speak life to each other when loved ones leave.

(Osagie) Leave like leaves in fall. Love will be upheld no matter what season and I am convinced I'm not day dreaming- this will be done because God is love and He is who we depend on.

(LaTavya) I need him to know, to love God because if He does not love God, he cannot love me.
He has to love me as he loves his own body.

(Osagie) So upon this foundation, I say - I just want to cradle myself in the crevice of your dimple and breathe in your essence so my heart may experience the aroma of heaven. I want to be your eternity. Abide with me forevermore. Let me warm you like your favorite sweater and be your nectar that tantalizes your intellectual palate…you like that sweater part don't you ☺?

(LaTavya) But can you give me special kind of love? Give me that love that has strings attached.
That love that makes even Cupid's arrows collapse.

(Both) The love that says if you had to choose the one you'd love to love, it would be me.

(LaTavya) Give me the kind of love that turns my cries into laughs
That easy, comfortable, messy hair, kisses amidst morning breath kind of love.
Be my Boaz so I can be your Ruth
That 1st Corinthians 13 is the love I want to give you
Give me that kind of love that even time cannot decay.
The kind of love that feels like we're always on
replay…replay…replay
Of the moment I first laid eyes on you, the moment you first smiled my way.
Give me your jokes over broken promises.
Give me your lifetime, your forever
I'll make sure you never

Have to wonder how much you mean to me.
I'll remind you daily

(Osagie) I've heard it said that God rested on the 7th day. I guess all I'm trying to say is that I want to be your 7th day. Come, rest. I'm not saying you're God, but you are God-breathed. You are God-sent; so, be my earth. I just want to plant within and be birthed again to be the man I know I'm meant to be. "Create in me a new heart Lord." Entail the details of the Creator's hand, making precise movements through your love, engraving deep in the unsettled cement in my soul. Awaken my soul to another wonder of love so surreal, I peer deep into your eyes and innocently inquire - are you real?

(Both) Because such a nourishing love feels like poems written to our very own cadence.

(Osagie) That favorite song

(LaTavya) That favorite home cooked meal kind of love.
Give me unfailing, give me undeniable, give me ideal

(Osagie) Can you give me submission?

(LaTavya) I will give you submission.

(Osagie) I need respect.

(LaTavya) I will give you respect.

(Osagie) I will pray for you. I will cover you.

(LaTavya) I will pray for you. I will give you real.

(Osagie) This Agape is one with my soul so I lay my will down to uphold you my crown, my glory, my beauty, my love to be my wife.

(Both) This is the love I seek.

Pause for the Cause

Satan is real, and you need to know this because you cannot recognize an enemy's schemes or defeat an enemy if you don't know you have an enemy. Satan roams this Earth seeking whom he can devour. He comes to kill, steal and destroy.

No matter how many times you hear it, it still remains the truth – the enemy has no interest in disturbing those who straddle the fence, who are entangled in sin, who rebel against the Word of God. Unless they turn from their ways of error, they are already where Satan wants them – lost, counted amongst those who will lose their way into the Book of Life, counted amongst those who rejected the free gift of salvation.

Satan's mission is to discourage, deceive, tempt, and attack those who trust in God, who draw closer to God, whose destination is eternal life because he is at war with God, and he wants us to lose our seal. But God is faithful and able to protect us, provide for us, and keep us from falling away. All we have to do is believe in Christ Jesus through faith, and by His grace, He will save us.

You know, when I was outside of the will of God, I went through some gloomy times, and I had my bouts of misery and let me tell you that it was a dark, fearful time. God did not know me. His promises did not cover me. Now, by faith and by God's grace, I live within His will. I still have afflictions and trials, but knowing that I can rest on God's promises makes those trying times so much easier to bear because His peace is unsurpassable, His love is unfailing, His grace abounds, His mercies are new each day, and His promises are my comfort. We have victory over every wicked scheme, every deceptive act, and every temptation in the name of Jesus.

Keep On Holding On
Hebrews 10:23

I was raised by my great, great grandmother and no matter how often things went wrong,
She'd always say, Baby, you just keep on holding on.
Whether I was 16 and telling her I was pregnant
Whether I lost a best friend, there was cancer or a death,
It was always the same thing. Baby, we just gone keep on holding on.
And as I would cry myself to sleep with my head planted on her shoulder,
She'd just reach over and say, "You may not understand it now, but you will when you get older."
She didn't do much explaining. You just had to take her word for it.
She'd say, "If I tell you an elephant is coming down the street, you'd better put your foot on it."

So, it wasn't until I was in my 20s that I learned why she would say just keep on holding on.
Because there will be times when you want to let go.
There will be times when you think you'd be better off doing things your way.
At least that way, you won't have to wait
For what will seems like an eternity for God's way to take place.
Because there will be times when it seems as if God has hidden His face.

Thorns will plant themselves in your side and afflictions will manifest.
Your faith, your patience, and your kindness will be put to the test.

There will be times when the midnight hours seem to stretch
And that joy in the morning, it will seem pretty farfetched.
You will labor and you will be heavy laden and still seem to find no rest.

Worry, doubt, guilt, shame – they will try to consume you
Failure and disappointment – they will tag along, too.

Sometimes, you may cry so much that your eyelids swell.
Other times, you will question what have I done to warrant such Hell.
You may get knocked down so much that kneeling
Becomes your new way of sitting.

But like my granny would say, Keep on holding on.
Because you just aren't strong enough to handle any of this alone.

You see, whomever seeks the kingdom of God, the enemy seeks to destroy.
And nothing angers the enemy more
Than a willful dedication to our Lord.

So, the adversary, He is seeking you to devour.
But when you hold on, you ignite an exclusive power
A power that comes only by the grace of God.

For even when you feel God is a far ways in the distance.
He is not a man that He should lie. He will still keep his promises.

So keep on holding on.
So you can run and not grow weary, walk and not faint.
So you can be portioned His renewed strength.

He will never leave you or forsake you.
Since He is for you, no weapon can prosper against you.

You keep holding on
Because the days hardest to bear, they will never come.
You will realize that your good days, they outweigh your bad ones.

We learn that the testing of your faith produces patience.
Patience produces character and character produces hope.
We hold on because we just simply can't afford to let go.

I'm in my 30s now and I'm like Paul, I have believed,
Therefore I speak.
If you let go of God, you leave God's presence.
But remember that any day in God's presence is better than a thousand days anywhere else.

So, you keep holding on.
When he speaks, it is done.
When he commands,
It stands fast.
The Lord is your refuge, your very present help in trouble.
The Lord is your light and your salvation, you shall not be afraid.
The Lord is your strong tower, you will be safe.
The Lord is your shepherd, you shall not want.
You just gotta keep on holding on.

For those thorns, His grace is sufficient.
For those afflictions, He's got your deliverance.
He's got your peace, your rest, your salvation, your joy
Your breakthrough. He's got all your reward.
Your job is just to keep on holding on.
Your job is to be still and know that God is God and He is God alone.

Here Is Christ
Romans 8:37

There are some of us whose plum colored smiles do one heck of a job hiding our brokenness.
Whose foundation powder and eye shadow overshadow our heavy, unbearable burdens?
Below those crisp tapered fades, those wristwatches and precisely placed scarfs,
And underneath our picture perfect facades
Are mental and emotional scars.
There are others who are desperately trying to forget our pasts, forget our mistakes
Trying to escape
The captivity from guilt, hurt and shame
There are even some of us who think we are just one long night away
From never seeing the morning sun.

So for you, if any of you be these I've described,
If I could give you one thing that could save your life
I would give you Christ.
For by even the hem of His garment, we are healed.

And I don't come with any similes or profound metaphors
No fancy, 6 syllable academic words,
I'm just gonna give you the Scriptures.
"Thus saith the Lord."

Bring Him your brokenness, and He will repair, reshape and restore you
Give Him your burdens, and He will give you His rest
Bring him your afflictions
He will trade you His deliverance
He will take your past and dispense His forgiveness

He will remove your guilt, hurt and shame, and replace them with His peace.
Bring Him your presumed defeat, and He will allocate your victory.
He'll assign joyful mornings for your midnight hours
You have weakness, He's got strength and power.

Give Him your Goliaths, your 9 foot giants, and he will give you the courage of David.
Give him your fiery furnace
And He will be your fourth person.

Nebuchadnezzar spake, "Did we not tie up three men and throw them into the fire? Look! I see four men, loosed, walking around."
The king called for them to come, and when the three Hebrew boys came out,
Their hair was not singed, the fire had not even destroyed their clothes,
Neither did they smell of smoke.
So commit to him your obedience
And He will distribute His protection.

And if you battle with any sins
He's still got those nail prints.
A pierced side
A back filled with stripes

And I don't only speak from what I've read; I speak as a witness
Of what I've seen, heard and experienced.

For our transgressions, our iniquities,
His body was stretched across an old rugged tree

So, if you let me point you to the one who can save your life.
Here He is. I give you Christ.

The Name of Jesus
John 14:2-3

There is power in the name of Jesus.
Power that makes even the darkness recede
So His name will be on my lips continually
Flowing ever so sweetly

Power that makes even the waves
And the winds obey
That heals the sick, casts out demons, gives sight to the blind
Makes the lame to walk, restores the dead back to life
That makes a whole lot out of just a little
And takes wretched men and transforms them into disciples
There is power in the name of Jesus.

Our only way to the Father.
Immanuel, the very name that means God with us.
The name above all names.
The only name by which we can be saved.
The name of the Perfect One who came down just to take our place.

The name of Jesus.

Betrayed by a kiss
Denied by a follower of His
Beaten, mocked, insulted, spat upon, pierced,
Led like a lamb to the slaughter
To die, cursed upon a tree in Golgotha.

But I heard a singer say, "That's not how the story ends!"
3 days later, He rose with all power in His hands
Power that causes us to be born again.
That saves us, preserves us until the end.
Jesus did not rot in some grave. His is risen!

Death is swallowed up in victory, the serpent's head is crushed
Corruption puts on incorruption
He has overcome this world
We will study war no more

Jesus, the one who is soon to come a second time
The one who gives us access to the Book of Life
Wonderful Counselor, Mighty God, Everlasting Father, Prince of Peace
Alpha and Omega, First and Last, Beginning and the End.
Mediator, Deliverer, Healer
Redeemer, Jesus our Savior.

No more crying, no more sorrow, no more curse, and no more pain
No more slanderers, murderers, no more liars, and no more heartbreak
No more infidelity
No more too much month at the end of your money
No more prisons, no more flawed education systems
No more police brutality, no more racism
No more your black aint good enough
No more depression, no more deception,
No more hunger or homelessness
No more evil, no more death

There is more than enough room in my Father's house. If it were not so, I would have told you.
I go to prepare a place for you and when everything is ready, I will come and get you so that where I am, you also may be

There is reconciliation
There is salvation
There is power in the name of Jesus.

FOR BOOKING PLEASE CONTACT LATAVYA FOSTER AT poetjustay@gmail.com

www.ingramcontent.com/pod-product-compliance
Lightning Source LLC
Chambersburg PA
CBHW031213090426
42736CB00009B/895